Thanks to the women that allowed this book to take off. From sensitive topics, hitting home, the smiles, and even the tears; I can say that I have a lot of valuable information that I'm eager to share. Information comes directly from the 500+ men and women that were interested in being interviewed. Now I will warn you; you will read about different opinions from both our men and women that could make you think, question and even second guest your original way of thinking; but that's the beauty of reading. That's what makes this book better than the rest. Just know that all of my findings will leave you and your friends in suspense!!!

It's an honor knowing YOU were one of the one's that decided to support me.

-Datedocta

Understanding Her

 **Page 4**: The "W" Types of Women

 **Page 102**: The "O" ccupation in Women

 **Page 116:** The "M" aturity in Women
    a. *Rational v. Irrational Decisions*
    b. *Mind Choices v. Heart Choices*

 **Page 134:** The "A"ddition to Women
How she loves v. What she needs

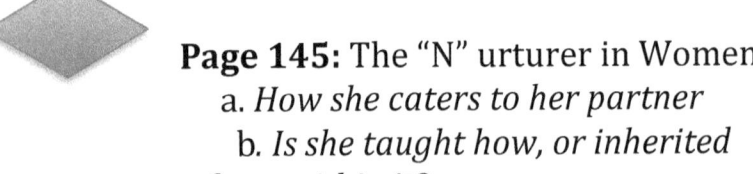 **Page 145:** The "N" urturer in Women
    a. *How she caters to her partner*
    b. *Is she taught how, or inherited from within it?*

 **Page 149**: Final Thoughts

Lets just say you are in for a treat!! For the first time, a male has placed on his thinking cap to speak for the males out there who are eager in understanding a woman. Now, I will admit, it will be a lot of information, but well worth it throughout the entire book. Please spread the word about this book to others. Feel free to post your opinion on social media, my personal website below, or even via word of mouth. Buckle your seat belt and get ready for the ride of lifetime in this book like no other!!!!!!

Website: www.Datedocta.com

Enjoy!

"W"

Are you ready ladies and gents for what I have to say? Reader discretion is advised! On a daily basis we hear about if there's ever been a book written about how to understand a woman. We constantly hear that women are hard to understand, they're hard to please, and that women are a part of their own tax bracket. My passion is to answer those questions now, but through action. Keep it simple; a woman is a person that biologically has different physical features than the average man. When you are blessed with different physical features, it increases the chances of you articulating things much different than those of a different physical presence. It's like questioning why a 5'6 man has a tough time touching the backboard of a 10-foot rim, than someone that's 7'2. These two have different extremities that

Understanding Her

hinder one from having an easier time accomplishing the task. Starting with the "Why," just with understanding and passing any type of test, you have to understand a great percentage of what's being explained in order to increase the chance in understanding the material. Now, the less you learn and/or understand, the likelihood of passing the course/test decreases tremendously.

The "Why" is what's going on with the woman in question. Remember, women are different than men, but only in specific categories. Why? Why? Why? The "Woman" stems all the way back in the biblical times of "Adam & Eve."

> ***The woman is depicted upon the decision that was made between "Adam & Eve" with the tree of life. How would the world have been if Adam had not eaten from such tree?***

Understanding Her 6

Remaining in the biblical days, women were viewed as those that had children for their significant other(s) or others for the purpose of breeding. In this day in age women were viewed as being just the homemaker, with no intent of bringing any other form of financial backing to the table; outside of what the man brings. Women were viewed as nurturers during this time, which also meant that the following roles were expected:

- **Bathing children**
- **Making babies**
- **Keeping the house cleaned**
- **Cooking meals for everyone**
- **Managing the home**
- **Remaining faithful to her partner**
- **Available sexually**
- **Superwoman**
- **Laundry**

Here are some of the things that women were not allowed to do, and/or frowned upon for even considering:

-Working

-Being disobedient to their partners

-Frequent public outings

-Provocative clothing

-Infidelity

-The ability to voice her opinion either in public or in contradiction of her better half.

    All of this talk about how a woman is expected and/or perceived in helping others, what about how she's to be treated? The woman is expected to be treated as a queen!! Reason being is that the world has created her as such. The world has created her as a special person that is to be within the rib of her partner. The specialty in her is to assist within her home as the primary backbone of the home. With that type of specialty, why would you want to treat her any other way? Women are created in resembling flowers that are watered to see blossom. A flower requires loving, watering, praising and even cherishing towards appreciation. Any other way is considered irrational and/or irrelevant for a woman's sake. As concerning as it may sound about the other ways of a woman's resemblance, you'd be surprised the ways some of us have chosen to water this type precious flower once a month, as oppose to weekly visits. No worries, we'll get into more depth in the proceeding chapters about the "queen" in a woman and how she should be treated by the partner.

    In the bible we tend to see that a woman's role is to be submissive to her man. What's submissive? Submissive is someone that respectfully takes direction from her dominant partner at times in the home, daily functions, and frequent relationship/marriage endeavors. Not to be confused or misconstrued with a dictator; submissive has nothing to do with control, but with compromising for the sake of benefiting on both ends of the love spectrum. Being that a woman was viewed as being submissive in the home, she was still able to be "co-dependent" of taking care of her own personal responsibilities as well. Such term is sometimes used as being helpless or inability to fend for self; but that's not the case here. Such term is designed to be a helpful partner, while being able to cater to self as need be. What's co-dependent? Co-dependent is the ability of both parties to work together to accomplish multiple relationship bound/singular concerning things that can successfully assist both parties.

    Moving forward from the biblical times to the early 1900's, things have changed for the taking. Reason being is that so much has occurred over the past few decades that's put women in not only a different bracket of thinking, but also a different tax bracket financially. Here are some of those things:

-Women are starting to work smaller setting jobs

-Laws are being formulated in protection of our women and their rights to be protected as human beings

-Women are beginning to voice their opinions within group setting

-Women are beginning to contribute more within the home financially

-Women are beginning to hire help in the home to complete duties that were once assigned to do by women

-Women are beginning to participate and orchestrate in legalized protest

-Feminist groups are beginning to formulate

Understanding Her

-We're starting to see more women within the educational system in charge of teaching

With everything that's beginning to transform now, you have to ask yourself; "What happens next with the genetic make-up of women? Does the new "woman" begin changing her identity? Do we, as guys have to learn new and improved ways on treating our women now? Or what? Now, I'm not saying that with the new things that are circulating within the benefit of women is a bad thing, but what I am saying is that, does the dynamics of how to now treat our women need to change for guys to now adapt to the new and improved woman?

So, lets move 20 years into the future from the early 1900's, to the mid 1900's where equal rights have now become established prematurely for both parties. We now have equivalent laws in place where both parties can contribute similar attributes in the home. At this time,

Understanding Her

things begin to happen. We begin seeing what was once the submissive partner, has now become equally yoked as the co-primary partner. Do such partnership cause issues in the new day in age from the mid 1900's to now? I've done a lot of chatting up to this point, now lets hear some of what you have to say. Here are a few questions I would like to run by you. I'll be sure to leave enough room for my long-winded writers:

1. Do you feel that with the new laws in place pertaining to equal rights, it decreases the chances of the man being the head of his household?

_____
_____
_____
_____
_____
_____
_____.

13 Understanding Her

2. Do you feel that if relationships remained within the "submissive" state of mind as it once was centuries ago, the world have been extremely dull, or similar to what it's transformed into now?

_____
_____
_____
_____
_____
_____
_____
_____
_____
_____
_____.

3. **(A woman only question)** Do you feel that this day in age could possibly withstand the image of the woman centuries

ago with being super submissive to her man?

_____
_____
_____
_____
_____
_____
_____
_____
_____.

4. In this day in age, could the world survive off only having the male species as the head of all business, legal matters, and governmental functions?

_____
_____
_____
_____
_____
_____

Understanding Her

_____
_____.

5. Do you feel that since the world has stepped away from the spiritual foundation of roles in the home, that it could decrease the chances of success in marriages?

_____
_____
_____
_____
_____
_____
_____
_____.

The next part of the "W" that we'll focus on will be the "why" she is the way she is. Women are designed to be loved by many. Women are designed to give off the essence to others that shows why she should be loved, how she should be loved, and the steps it takes to have her love proven to her. Women are created for the sake of being embraced by others, including her for the most part. Women are designed to be cherished, loved, catered to like no other, and to be beautified like a man's precious or valuable asset in his life. Women are created to be appreciated by any and all that are either interested in her intimately, from a family approach, or at least within her own emotional place of comfort. Think about it for a second; a woman's features includes things that places her in a position to be loved in different ways then that of a man:

-Breast-

-Smooth skin

-Long hair

-The female fragrance

-Emotionally sensitive

-Loveable

-Soft voice

-Emotion at times

-The vagina

-The ability to wear make-up

Keeping hair in tip top shape

-The list continues

    As you can see from the list, these things signify many areas that focus on some of the most intimate features within a woman today. These things are very precious or either requires a soft touch within or on a woman. For my guys that are reading this book; nowhere did you see where I put aggression or force within the list on being loved by others. Now, I do realize that sexual preference can be mixed in with a little aggression and etc, but the initial part of love is a completely different category that I'm focusing on now. Good try though (Haha)
Why is she the way she is? She's the way she is because of the following things:

- Genetic Make-up
- Inherited traits from parents
- Her environment
- Her associates
- Social media
- Her past
- How she unconsciously chooses to be
- The music she chooses to listen to

As you can see, the above things that can sometimes dictate the future influence in women. As it can for a man, such things can play a huge impact on any and all that choose to embrace such characteristics. Now, what the world has been waiting on; what's this I keep hearing about the "7 Types of Women" in the world? The world consists of 7 types of women that we're amongst everyday. Each of the women that I'm getting ready to discuss all have either suffered or progressed from many different occurrences in life. Many things in life have defined women in some form or fashion. Now you will always hear in life that you shouldn't allow what has happened in the past to dictate you future; but in the real world that would mean that you're perfect and that you should prepare to throw the first stone. Think about it for a second. I'll wait... The world consists of the following women:

1. ***Independent Issabella***

2. ***Debby Dependent***

3. ***Insecurity Levine***

4. ***Conswella Control***

5. ***Co-Co Co-Dependent***

6. ***Constance Confrontation***

7. ***Boyish Brenda***

Here shortly we will begin chatting about the 7 types of women that are amongst us in the world, along with how we as partners can manage to date either one. You'd be surprised some of the things we tend to avoid asking and/or considering when dating a person. Lets just say you'll begin doing so after this next section. Good luck...

7 Types of Women

Independent Issabella

Welp, lets start with the first type of woman out there; "The Independent Issabella." This woman is the definition of a "solo go getter" that strives for success, for independence, for the drive of not depending on anyone for any reason, and the type of enjoying having her own. This type of woman is one that usually spends a great amount time working on her own personal, financial, spiritual and physical goals all by her lonesome. Now, there's nothing wrong with some of the things I suggested about "The Independent Issabella," but pay attention to the person she's spending the majority of her time with. Pay attention to the time she dedicates on associating with loved ones and friends. Pay attention to the energy she puts in with catering to her one and only star player; that's right, HER! Pay attention to the enjoyment in life of it only being about her. Pay attention to the first set of letters that each word of this title begins with. In the bible it talks about being fruitful. In the bible it talks about being social and catering to your own vessel in life, as well as others. It also talks about the difference in what the mind or heart can do to your decision making methods if you choose to neglect either feature. Lets do a little dissecting.

Striving for independence?

There's nothing wrong with striving to be a better person in life, but does it become an issue when you desire to be a one-man/woman show? As people, we're designed to be mindful, peaceful, humble, oriented with people, and designed to work together to achieve team spirited goals. Still striving to be independent? I've found that when we step outside of how we're originally designed, then it increases the chances of tension in our psyche. Tension in our own psyche does exactly what it sounds like; causes excessive tension in our psyche. Excessive tension eventually turns into anti social cues; and you know the rest. Lets dig a little deeper. When you hear about someone that's independent, it makes you think that a person tends to want to do things by themselves. When you think of someone who's independent, you tend to think that someone prefers to take over everything, refuses help, makes their own money, calls their own shots, and the list continues. Remember what I said, as individuals, we're designed to develop a team approach in all that we do. Having that team approach increases the chances of having a more successful business adventure; but as an independent issabella, some may never know.

What are the DON'TS OF ISSABELLA?

When we think of the don'ts or the negative side of the *issabella,* we think of the following:

-Refusing to ask for help

-Would rather struggle, and then seek assistance
-A one-man/woman army

-Confrontational

-Very guarded at times

-Good chance of being single

-Has an opinion about everything

-The infamous "know it all."

-The one that'll work 23 hours a day

-Is her own therapist and psychiatrist

-Constantly gives reasons as to why she doesn't need a man.

-Lack of social skills

-Tends to choose work over play

-Distant from family at times

-Issues with being told what to do

As you can see, the list can go on and on. Being independent has a lot of negative attributes about it that cannot only make you distant yourself from others, but it can also cause others not to want to socialize with you.

Issabella in a Relationship?

Understanding Her

And then there was Issabella trying to fall in love. No worries, I'll take it easy in this category. Now imagine all of those features I've just mentioned in the previous text about the independent woman; compare those to being in a relationship for a second. Can you imagine the possible struggle of it? Can you imagine how much work invested that it could take? Could you imagine the type of guy it could take to perfect this style of a relationship? Could you imagine the discussions? Lets chat for a second. I'm going to throw out a few questions for you.

1. "Not asking for help" is one thing, but what happens when you revert back to the role of a man and his duties to be the head of the household while dating someone in the "independent" category?

   _____
   _____
   _____

Understanding Her

_____
_____
_____.

2. Dating this type of a woman, would it be wise for her to date someone that demands being the head, or someone that doesn't mind her taking account of things where she's strongest at and allowing her to be a possible overseer?

_____
_____
_____
_____
_____
_____
_____
_____.

3. Something to think about it? Back to her not asking for help: what if she's dating a guy that enjoys helping his woman? Do you think it could decrease the

27   **Understanding Her**

chances of the guy feeling masculine?

_____
_____
_____
_____
_____
_____
_____
_____
_____
_____.

Who knows! There are so many questions a person can ask at this time, but I'll leave room for you to think a little bit. The next one focuses on her preferring to struggle, rather than asking for help. Such features could cause so much drama and unwanted issues in a relationship. It can get to the point of hurting herself, possible eviction of valuable things in her life, or even jail time. Such characteristic can be very scary when it comes to being in a committed relationship. Such characteristics can cause her credit score to constantly drop by not receiving help to make payments on time. It could cause issues with being open about things in her mind. It could cause trust issues. What about the confrontational parts of Issabella? When it comes to being confrontational, you'll begin seeing a lot of these issues that will generate from being told what to do, thinking that her man or woman is trying to challenge her or somehow doubting her intelligence in some way. Now, we could go through each of the characteristics of this portion of dating issabella, but I want you to hear all of the other details of understanding HER.

But, How Do I Date Issabella?

Before you begin dating this woman, make sure she has officially called it off with the one person she is magically in love with the most; herself. Now, there's nothing with her loving herself like no other, but the issue comes in when it becomes difficult for you to see past that star player in you, while neglecting to love others. Some of the other things you have to check on are the reasons that have driven her in being the person she is today; possibly being forced in not depending on others, the desire to do things for self and only self, the desire in looking out soley on the best interest of self, and no desire in taking accountability on things. Now I will provide a disclaimer in this section as you have some guys that prefer this type of woman and will fall head over hills for her. The independent woman is one that thousands of guys strive on seeking and will do everything possible to find her. Once she has made efforts in tweeking these minor setbacks, then she is ready to get back on the market for dating again. Your job is to understand, embrace, and to apply these things I've mentioned to you today; not to provoke them based on the type of woman you demand her to be. Besides, no

Understanding Her

one is putting a gun to your head to date her.....

hmmmmm..........

Debby Dependent

Now, here's one that's a bit different than what we've just focused on; "Mrs. Debby Dependent." This young lady is one that tends to be frowned upon by many. This person is one that's semi respected, but also hated upon. Lets discuss the definition of the "Debby Dependent." She is the one that's dependent upon everyone around her. She's the one that expects everyone else to do things for her, as oppose to what she can do for them. She's the one that has to have someone present in order to make her ends meet. Her ends are in reference to financial and emotional needs. This person is one that emotionally refuses to get out there and work just as hard as the next person. This is the person that refuses to sacrifice her time for labor or financial gain. This is the person that would rather spend the money, as oppose to working for it. This is the person that has a history of taking

Understanding Her

advantage of other people for her own gain. What's another name for this type of person that we've heard a few times in songs? You've guessed it, "Gold Digger," by Kanye West. Ready for my famous questions just yet?

1. Have you ever dated someone that fits into the category and if so, why did you stay knowing such characteristics were present?

   _____
   _____
   _____
   _____
   _____
   _____
   _____.

2. Do you feel that because society paints a picture that guys are to flaunt money to receive women, which it's disrespectful, it's ok for us guys to become offended

when the woman acts exactly as to how we wanted her to respond? (besides, we wanted her to be like us for our money right?)

_____
_____
_____
_____
_____
_____
_____
_____
_____.

3. Do you think that if we flaunted things in addition to money, that the odds of gold diggers becoming extinct could happen?

_____
_____
_____
_____
_____
_____

Understanding Her   34

_____
_____
_____
_____
_____
_____.

What are the Don'ts of Debby?

What about the DON'TS of her now? When we think of the don'ts or the negative side of the *Debby Dependent,* we think of the following:

-Someone that's been taught to depend on others

-Someone that prefers to be catered to, as oppose to returning the favor to the partner

-Using their partner for financial gain

-Starting arguments to avoid contributing

-Being spoiled from a young age to adulthood

-Unconsciously feeling as though she has to be taken care of by her partner

-Financially attracted to partners with a specific salary

-Not motivated to contribute to the table

-Not as attracted to those who do not meet a specific salary cap

-Struggles to love for the right reasons

-Tends to fall in lust easily

-Tends to have the best fashion

-Has the most enemies

-Portrayed as a very promiscuous person

-Issues with being very naïve towards the request of her partial significant other.

Understanding Her 36

As you can see, the list can continue with the discrepancies of the "Dependent Debby." You have to be careful when you're dealing with someone that's in this category of a woman. This style of a person is very manipulative at times, but also naïve. This type of a woman tends to flock to any man that can somewhat provide her with a financially stable life. The real trick is, I wonder if she would put up a front to convince the man/partner that she's interested? That's the kicker right now. The real question now is, "How can we tell the difference in whether she wants you for the right, or wrong reasons? I'll let you answer that one below:

1. How do we figure out the ways in deciphering if she's being honest or telling a story?

   _____
   _____
   _____
   _____

_____
_____
_____
_____.

Debby in a Relationship?

When it comes to her being in a relationship, it can become tricky. Tricky meaning that it may be difficult to see either the truth or the deceit in her when she's dependent upon on you. Men are designed to be providers, protectors, and the best friend of his better half. A man is designed to feel loved, wanted and appreciated by his better half. It can become mindboggling when he has a tough time knowing if the partner he's with is willing to be a co-dependent of what he brings to the table, or is only using him for what he can bring, and could leave if it subsides. That's where it can become tricky. Now within this type of woman, it could potentially be a better fit for some. Reasons for saying this is because the church teaches us that women are to be submissive to a man that can lead them into the right direction. The church teaches us that guys should find a soul mate that can be the back bound of our success. The church wants us to have someone that can be the stemming rib to our rib cage. The church also talks about the man finding one that can cater just as much to him, as he can to her. Uh oh, another question just hit me!!!

> 1. Is it safe to say that a "dependent debby" person has a higher success rate of molding into that church driven mentality of who's a better fit for him than any other choice? (Hmm, something to think about)

_____
_____
_____
_____

_____
_____
_____.

But, How Do I Date Debby?

Well, with this type of woman you have to be very careful. Think about it this way, this is a woman that is portrayed as being very dependent upon you. This is a woman that is sometimes portrayed as wanting to take advantage of you if you allow her to. This is a woman that may not have as much educational background to necessarily support herself, which then may give reasons as to why you might be the type in pushing her to seek you. With this type of woman, my advice is to be mindful and aware of her intent. When doing so, you're able to better prepare yourself as to whether you want to supply her of these gold-digging needs, or to allow someone else to take on that responsibility. Once you've decided to allow her into your life, you then have no right to complain due to knowing how she plans to operate. Besides, you knew when you saw the signs that the vision wasn't clear; you just chose to wipe the window thinking it would vanish.

Hmmmmm......

Many of us will flaunt our money to these women, but will turn around and be pissed when that's all she views us as; a flaunter..

Insecurity Levine

I would like to apologize in advance to my readers for this section. It will be the longest due to "Insecurities" playing a huge role in this type of woman. Insecurities come in many different fashions that it's interesting to hear about. An insecurity is a way of thinking, acting, and feeling towards particular issues in life that have caused us to struggle in managing. Insecurities come into play when we've been both emotionally and morally injured to the point of losing a bit of faith and trust in either a person or us. Insecurities can sometimes separate us from either having a successful relationship leading up to marriage, or it could be the reason you emotionally choose not to trust even your own self in moving forward with a person. Insecurities stem from the following issues in life:

-Being cheated on

-Not being able to trust people

-Physical abuse

-Emotional abuse

-Being with a compulsive liar

-Sexually assaulted

-Not loving self

-Being overweight/underweight

-Being criticized by others

-Lack of motivation

-Not feeling appreciated by others

-Control issues

-Falling quickly in love

-The list continues…

The next thing that we're going to focus on will be the Don'ts of the Levine. This category will be about some of the things we see when dating/married to those with insecurities. In this category, we tend to see issues that lead to divorce, physical or emotional abuse, and so much more.

The Don'ts of Levine?

-Quick to accusing others of cheating

-Afraid to date others

-Struggles in sleeping

-Choosing to return the favor by doing others wrong

-Keeping your guard up when dating

-Blaming others for your issues, as oppose to taking accountability

-Self Doubt

-Fear of working on issues with self both emotionally and spiritually

-Tends to have more family driven issues than others

-Constant need for assurance of self

-Tends to have low self worth

-Tends to have low self-esteem

-Tends to be more tearful

- Subconsciously attracted to others that will treat them wrong

And much more...

With that being said, insecurities will follow any and every person if that person refuses to work on the insecurity in a timely fashion. No matter the issue, it has the ability to take over the mind in ways unimaginable. Whether it is in reference to dating, or overcoming stressful events, an insecurity will be tough to overcome, but removable. Now, lets focus a bit on the dating/marriage side of things.

Is Levine ready for the dating game?

Levine is just as ready as she would like to be. Now I will admit, Levine will have a tough time dating and/or marrying someone if she has yet to work on her insecurities. Remember some of things I mentioned that come with these insecurities? Whether you do or not, those issues can and will lead to her being more in depth with her own troubles if nothing is done or catered to for a better her; TRUST ME! One of the basic things we see in those of the "insecurity caliber" doing is treating others that ways they've been treated. Starting with being cheated on; sometimes, but not often, you'll see a great amount of women that were mistreated this way and have decided to not allow anyone else to beat them to the punch of cheating on them first, so they'll typically decided to do it to any and every person that steps foot in her path of loving her. Unfortunately it's the truth in her that sees this act or actions as being a "get back" at those that have wronged her,

Understanding Her

or another way in possibly coping for her own hurt. Sometimes you'll see women engaging in this act to avoid getting hurt again, or simply doing it to avoid getting into serious relationships in the future by appearing as the "whore type," as oppose of the wifey type." A woman in this caliber has the mindset that she would like the world to see how she's felt over the years of staying within something that wasn't healthy, but in her mind it was the next best thing than being single. Sometimes you'll see a woman who's experienced a chain of cheating partners more often than usual that she may return the favor of subconsciously assuming that he/she's going to cheat on her, so she may discreetly push him/her away "just because" without event knowing it. Sometimes we'll see other coping mechanisms where the woman may become very guarded and anxious about her partner cheating on her that she can become the typical "micro-manager" in her relationship. We've all experienced this supervisor that everybody hated because it meant that there was some sense of no trust to the point of having to be watched at all times. This is kind of like being in a correctional facility or a psych facility where 15-30 minute checks are in place for either your safety or the liability of staying employed. Another thing that could happen would be that she could constantly demand affirmation and/or confirmation that you're going to treat her right. Now, there's nothing wrong with having the conversation of the type of person you are and how well you plan to treat a person; but it can become concerning when the demand or need is there to constantly remind a person on how you're planning to treat them when the need of confirmation is present.

I think it's safe to say that we as people all have some form of insecurities in our souls that somewhat hinders us from making the best decisions out there. I would say that as people, we're nowhere near perfect. Insecurities can and will take over the mind frame if we allow it to.

Understanding Her

One other thing that was mentioned in this section was that of the "fear of working on issues." This portion will be a bit sensitive as it relates to the "Insecurity" category. The term "fear" itself can and will play a remarkable toile on the brain for sure. This term has the ability to prevent you from being successful, prevent you from conquering your fears, prevent you from being the real you, and preventing you from allowing happiness back into your life. When we add the fear into the dating life for "Levine," we have to be mindful that she may become afraid of being attached and/or becoming close to you. Reason being is that her past has shown her that you and the other entire potential partner are in it for one thing, and will lie about everything possible to retrieve that one thing; if it means selling both your soul and hers to get it. Dating someone that's fearful will be tough for sure, but not as bad when the fearful person has invested a little time for self to re-create self. Fear will be the reason she's afraid to trust you. Fear will be the reason she's concerned about telling you her deep and most dark secrets. Fear is the reason she's afraid to step forth into the church because she's tired of praying for you. Lastly, fear is the struggle she will face in either wanting to give you a chance, versus listening to her parents to take a break on dating for a while.

      The last thing I'll discuss about this type of woman will be the one filled with "Self Doubt." Yikes, this might be one of the key elements that hinders her from having successful relationships. Self-doubt is the difference in being successful or not. Self –doubt has the ability to stand in the way of you talking yourself into a success story. Self-doubt does exactly just that; it helps you doubt yourself to the point of keeping you from being you. Self-doubt is just that; it helps you ponder on everything that's designed to keep you from being great. Self-doubt can make or break you, if you allow it. The same energy you put into preventing yourself

Understanding Her

from being great could be the same energy you could use to put in writing the next billion-dollar business plan. Now, lets stay on track with this type of woman. Self-doubt plays so many mind games when it comes to dating someone with this type of issue. This issue would stand in the way of her believing in herself towards her own personal goals. When she feels this way about herself and her goals, she's likely to bring that negative energy into her relationship. When she has these negative thoughts about herself, the likelihood of her wanting it to be the same for her partner is high. A woman with this way of thinking could do one or two things in a relationship; she could subconsciously hope that her partner fails just like she did in her journey to success, or she could be the type that converts her energy in helping her partner to be successful because she didn't quite believe in her own dreams; and expect the same in return from her partner. You'd be surprised the energy we can put in helping others and how it could put our own selves in a billion dollar category. In this category of the woman, you will begin to see a lot of resentment, jealously, and envy between the woman and her partner. Reason being is that she obviously wanted to do better in her life then where she's at currently, but can't seem to develop the drive in doing so. It either gets worse for her when she's with someone that either has it all together and is striving for greatness and she's not, or better due to it turning into an eye opener because she's decided to allow his motivation to convert into her. Another toxic issue in the matter is if she's with someone that is struggling just as bad but has at least landed at a place where she wants to be so she criticizes him for that. What I mean by the last comment was that you may see women with guys that aren't as smart as she is, but have at least gone farther in life with a great success story in the making and it bothers her to a "T" because she feels like he should be struggling just as bad; THAT my friend is what we call an INSECURITY!!

> The same energy you put into preventing yourself from being great, could be the same energy you could put in writing the next billion-dollar business plan...

How Do I Date Her Now?

I'll keep it brief with you on this one. Just like any coach in practice with his players; he or she is going to ensure that his starting 5 is of the strongest that can perform at their peek, while the other issues are patiently wavered out during the sequence of the game with substitution. Compared to dating this young lady, you have to go back to the practice sessions and see if she's emotionally ready for the dating world. Many of the lovely ladies today have been hurt so bad that it's difficult for them to somewhat look past the past. Most women that were unfortunately exposed to a life of emotional anguish, verbal abuse, and infidelity have a tough time trusting and/or overcoming the insecurity issues that are followed by these unfortunate acts. It's a must that you ensure that she's at least 55% over some of the unfortunate things that may have happened. The other 45% is for you as her partner to improve with the ideations of doing better overall for her. The next thing to do is to check her self worth. Begin asking questions that detect if she loves herself. Ask questions to see what goals she may have in life and what steps she's taking to reach those goals. Another thing you'll need to figure out is her level of accountability in life. There's no worst feeling than getting to know a person that struggles with accountability or at least has issues with not seeing that it's an issue. Another thing you can begin paying attention to is how she speaks about her past and whether or not she shows great emotion pertaining to those past experiences. The last thing that I encourage my people to do is to ensure that she's both physically and emotionally capable in loving you the way you respectfully desire to be loved. Before I let you leave, I want to run a few questions by you:

1. Could you date a woman that's not completely over her past?

   _____
   _____
   _____
   _____
   _____
   _____
   _____.

2. Have you ever dated a woman that required constant redirection of her emotional instabilities?

   _____
   _____
   _____
   _____

_____
_____
_____
_____
_____
_____
_____
_____.

3. If you had to choose between the two, which one would it be: dating a woman with trust issues, or a woman that doesn't believe in herself?

_____
_____
_____
_____
_____
_____
_____
_____
_____.

Understanding Her 56

Hmmmm……..

Conswella Control

And then there was the controlling type! Not to be alarmed, we're going to approach multiple angles during this section of the book. This type of woman has so many avenues of understanding that I would strongly encourage you to read this section a few times so that you don't miss a thing. Lets get started!!! Who exactly is "Conswella Control?" It's self-explanatory with this one; this is a person that has control issues within specific areas of her life, including her relationship and/or marriage. Many of us have had the pleasure, or torment in dating this woman in our lives. Whether it turned into a marriage, or even a divorce settlement; we have to be mindful of who it is we're pursuing or getting rid of. Not every person can handle such type. No disrespect intended on this type of woman. Women of this caliber are created from multiple ways in life such as:

-Finally leaving physically/verbally abusive relationships/marriages

-Having a controlling parent growing up in life; preferably the father figure

-Sometimes you'll see women in this category who have been exposed to sexual abuse and desire to control any future intimate relationships

-Associating self around very independently influential people that strongly promote female independence

-Being involved in a multitude of relationships where she needed to take charge due to a partner that wasn't emotionally and/or financially stable

-Having an independently-driven type of employment

-Having more masculine friends and/or family members

Now that we've gone over a few of the creations of this type of woman, what do you think? I'll wait.......

1. Have you ever dated/married someone that fits in this type of woman?

   _____
   _____
   _____
   _____
   _____
   _____
   _____
   _____.

2. Could two people independently-driven, possibly create happiness with one another?

   _____
   _____
   _____
   _____

_____
_____
_____
_____
_____
_____
_____
_____.

3. Can you turn her from the controlling type, to a more co-dependent type?

_____
_____
_____
_____
_____
_____
_____
_____.

Be sure to think about the above questions. Each of the said questions play a huge role into the possible success rate in relationships. Not everyone can handle and/or create a sense of happiness with this type of woman. Some women these days aren't able to recognize whether she has controlling issues until someone or a flock of "daters/friends" reveal it to her. Sometimes she'll refuse to hear that she has these issues and will confuse it with the need of being assertive. Sometimes she'll be the type to view it as knowing what she likes in life and doesn't want it any other way. Lastly, she'll view these controlling issues as a way of living a structured life, which leads me to the next question; what's the difference in being a structured person, versus being too controlling?

Structured vs.	**Controlling**
Organized, but willing to compromise for both parties	Organized, but to the point of demanding things one way or the highway

Considers things from a group effort	Considers one's own efforts
Great leadership skills	Great dictatorship skills
Loves unconditionally	Loves with specific conditions to some
Dates to accommodate both parties at times	Dates to accommodate society to ensure the relationship is ok to the people
Prefers things to be in order	Demands things to be in order
Communicates	Demands
Compromises	Manipulates

What about the don'ts of Conswella?

When dealing with a woman of this caliber, you have to be mindful of the following characteristics:

-She may want total control of everything

-She may be more argumentative than usual

-She may become more confrontational than usual

-She may desire to be the one "wearing the pants" in the relationship/marriage

-She'll show love in ways of controlling you to do more for her, as oppose to her doing for you

-Sometimes she'll meet a person that she's unable to control, and it usually makes her very uncomfortable

-She'll do everything possible to place the power of the relationship in her favor

Now back to explaining a few extra things. Sometimes in life we may meet people that enjoy the thrill of controlling others and also being in control. When this type of person meets or crosses paths with those are competing for the same task, you may see more of what society calls as "The Power Struggle." This term is a constant fight for power. This is a constant desire to being in charge. This is one of those that we see a lot in this day in age because so much has changed. Compared to the early 50's and so on, life and opportunities have become more equal for both genders. During the change in role expectations, we tend to see more women in more of the CEO or CFO categories. We're seeing those same women making societies preference of business in becoming more envious and competitive. (Disclaimer) I am in no way saying that a woman being in CEO or CFO positions is wrong.

Understanding Her

Is Conswella Ready For The Dating Game?

What a great question! Now, it will be a bit lengthy as I explain this question, but it's all fun and influential. Can conswella date again? Is there a particular guy that's out there that can be helpful for her? Is there still hope for Conswella during this type? Hmmm....Lets chat people!!! To be completely honest, it would depend heavenly on the guy she's interested in, and his intent on the role he intends to play in this relationship. Sometimes you may see the controlling type of a woman with a guy that's very humble, modest, soft-spoken, and receptive to the mentality of this woman and other instances of "not speaking up." From a man's opinions of whether or not she's ready to start dating; yes, as long as she's aware of some of her intentions and emotional desires to be either less controlling, or to locate a partner that doesn't mind the aggressive intent of this lovely woman.

But, How Do I Date This Woman?

Hmm. You don't just yet! Prior to even considering, you'll need to make sure she breaks up with herself first, and then you can begin to pursue her. By her breaking up with herself will increase the chances of her having and/or making time to get to know who you are as a person. Breaking up with herself will increase the chances of you having the chance to get and understanding the real love in her soul. Allowing her time to break up with herself shows you the true person she is. Now, you ask," How do I get her to break up with herself?" It's simple; you need to figure out if the controlling side is what you need in a person and if you can handle it to the point of not needing to tweak it. What I mean by this option is that a lot of us are in need of a bossy/controlling person in our lives and a small percentage of us guys actually enjoy the controlling aspect of it. Another option to consider is if you realize her controlling intentions would be an issue in moving forward with you; it's a must that you address those said issues from the jump. If you find it being an issue, you NEED to thoroughly explain to her that you are in no way a dictator, but someone that can be fair to any one that he shows an interest in. Mention to her that you were raised to somewhat be an effective leader in the household or intimate relationship. Mention to her that you would like to possible evaluate some of the strengths and weaknesses between the both of us so that we may embrace our relationship as a whole, as oppose to getting involved in a power struggle. What this method says to your woman is that you are not trying to control her, but it says you're ready to be an effective leader in the relationship and still desires to embrace both parties for success in the future of us. You and your "controlling party" now have a choice to make at this point; she can either morally consider it, or you guys could go your separate ways for a brighter future. No need to beat a dead horse if you don't have to. A great leader doesn't focus on what he/she can control, he/she focuses on benefiting all parties with consideration of everyone's strengths.

Hmmmmm……

"The Power Struggle." This term is a constant fight for power. This is a constant desire to being in charge

Understanding Her

I have a few questions for you!

1. Would dating a controlling type of woman bother you and why?
   _____
   _____
   _____
   _____
   _____.

2. If you encountered a woman that was controlling, how would you nip it in the bud, especially if were interested in her?
   _____
   _____
   _____
   _____
   _____
   _____.

3. What are some of the ways you feel turns a woman into the controlling type?

Co-Co Dependent

Next, we have the "Co-Co Dependent" type of woman. This type of woman is expected to be the ideal woman of interest. This woman is one that isn't dependent upon her man, she is in fact dependent upon helping the relationship overall. The co-dependent type of woman is one that supports herself, her man at times, brings just as much to the table as her man, respects the outcome of the relationship, is a big fan of roles/responsibilities in her relationship, and is more likely to be humble in both her appearance and her demeanor towards her partner.

Woman within this category are of the following caliber:

-Respectful towards both herself and the relationship

-History of catering to her man

-Traditionally has grown up in a 2 parent home

-Tends to have a drive to keep both herself and her significant other happy

-Tends to have a reasonably high self-esteem

-Tends to have more social skills than any other type of woman

-Tends to love hard

-Tends to have longer intimate relationships

-Tends to have a great personality

-Tends to be a "Daddy's Girl."

-Tends to have an equal amount of both guy friends and female friends

-Tend to have a very modest point of view towards life at times

-Tends to love on a level of how their significant other needs to be loved, as oppose to making up their own love style for the partner

Now, lets chat for a bit about this type of woman. The "Co-Co Dependent" woman so happens to be created equally compared to other women out there. This woman has just as many opportunities as the next woman has. This woman just so happens to be able to interpret and apply traits that are more suitable to the average guy. Sometimes this woman is explained and/or understood as someone who is deemed "submissive," or has no issue with being led in her home. This woman appears as the type that does not mind being led by a god-fearing man or woman of interest. This woman is one that tends to see the strengths in her significant other while embracing them to improve the relationship. This woman is the type that has no issue with opening up to her partner about the things that have troubled her in her life, while promising to work on and through these flaws. Now, I'm not going to advertise this woman as a perfect person, but I will advertise her as someone that is humble enough to view the relationship as half full. Now, I'm not going to say that she's not going to ever be cheated on or possibly be mistreated; but I will say that this woman usually has a different way in dealing with some of these issues that I'm discussing. This woman will more than likely deal with the heart ache from the person that maybe has done her wrong. She will more than likely be the one losing sleep and becoming tearful at night just thinking about these unfortunate matters; the real question now is, "How does she bounce back, and does she make it known that she's been hurt over the years through her future actions?" That's the difference in the "Co-Co" type, versus several of the other women that I'll be speaking about in the book.

What are the Don'ts of Co-Co?

Well, as you can see there isn't enough space to add any forms of "Don'ts" in this category because this woman is too much of the ideal wife to be. Now, I will admit, this woman does have limited traits of forgiving others too easy. As nice as this woman tends to be, sometimes the forgiving side of her can get in the way of others actually taken ownership or accountability of their actions. Sometimes this type of woman can allow too many people to run all over her by way of being too nice. With that being said, there isn't too many things to mention that would be deemed "Don't's" for the Co-Co Dependent type of woman!!!

How Do I Date The "Co-Co" Type?

This one isn't too tricky. Remember, this type of woman is one to keep. This is the type of woman that a lot of guys desire, but tend to push her into being evil. The real question here is, "Are you ready to date, I know she is?" This type of woman is loved by many, but hated by others that wish they could love again like she continues to do. This type of woman would be easy to date. This woman doesn't expect too much, more so just the request to be loved the way she desires. As complicated as it may seem and/or appear to love the other ladies I've mentioned, it may not be as much as a challenge towards the Co-Co type. The reasons it may not be as difficult is because this woman knows exactly what she wants in a guy. This woman knows exactly what it's going to take to make her happy. This woman will more than likely say and show you the way in catering to her. Not to be confused with being spoiled, but to know and/or understand what it takes to make her happy is the key to just about every success story. Rest assure that she will definitely return the favor.

BONUS FACTS OF "CO-CO."

-Unfortunately, she tends to be cheated on the most

-Has a higher chance of switching sexuality preferences

-Tends to love hard

-Hard to transition back once she cheats after constant heartache.

-Will exhaust every available option to make things work in her relationship

-Has a phenomenal personality

-Tends to be more submissive

-Will usually put her occupation on hold to cater to her partner.

Once again, this woman is one that's loved by many, but constantly overlooked because she isn't the "Bad & Boujee" type that many guys prefer. Guys, stop overlooking the good ones for the one's that look better on your coattail. It'll wear off in the end and then what do you have?

Understanding Her 78

hmmmmmmm……

Once again, this woman is one that's loved by many, but constantly overlooked because she isn't the "Bad & Boujee" type that many guys prefer.

Constance Confrontation

Here's where it gets interesting. I want you to think for a second, what goes through your mind when you hear "confrontation?" Such term makes you think about someone that's always fussing, fighting, arguing, and someone that tends to revert a basic conversation into a heated discussion. This term makes you think a bit on the following features; how a person struggles in taking accountability, issues with having conversation without it ending on a negative note, and always having their guard up. Now, from the outside looking in, we tend to see a person that's physically aggressive at all cost when we hear about the confrontational type. The confrontational type is that woman that feels the need and/or obligation to retaliate to those that either are a threat to her, or at least presents different ways to emotionally attack her. Here are some of the reasons "Constance" may feel like she needs to attack:

-Because she feels that others are challenging her intellectual abilities

-Because she feels that people are getting too close to the real truth about her

-Because she feels that people are judging her

-She feels that others around her are at a better place financially/emotionally than she is

-She feels that others are telling her what to do

-She feels that you're not taking her talents into consideration

-When she feels that you doubt her

-When she feels that she's unable to accomplish something she's worked so hard for

What I've learned in life is that when you think different, you do different things. When you act different, it usually means you thought about the ending result differently than the average person that considered another action from you. It's simple, we're all different in some form or fashion; what really matters is making sure that we continue to strive in making much better decisions than the previous day. Now, lets focus more on the "Confrontational" here.

What Are The Don'ts of Constance?

When we think of the "DON'T'S of life, it makes us think on the things that we should avoid. It makes us think on the areas that cause the average eyebrow to rise up a bit. Lastly, when we think of the DON'T'S, we finally think of the people we pray to god to help us learn to stay away from.

Understanding Her

At this time it's best that we become aware of those things that adds more fuel to the fire while dating the constance type. The don't's in life with this woman are of the following considerations:

-How she handles things both emotionally and physically

-How she caters to herself

-How she values herself

-What goals does she have in life?

-What are some of her triggers in life?

-What type of relationship did she have with her parents; preferably her dad?

-What are some of her defaulted defense mechanisms?

-What ways does she handle stressful situations?

Understanding Her

-What are the ways she fights with others?

-Does she have people in her life where she feels comfortable in actually being herself?

-Will she allow you to love her?

-And so many more questions to name

Ms Constance is a woman that has either been hurt emotionally, or raised in a lifestyle of constant verbal and/or masculine style intent. Ms. Constance over the years has shown the world that we all can respond and/or deal with things in life; but the choice to handle it a particular way is our choice from then. Now, many will view Ms. Constance as someone that always has her guard up no matter the obstacle; but have we ever considered the fact that she may be afraid? Have we ever considered the side effects of being afraid of something?

Understanding Her

Think about it for a second.... Imagine how you felt prior to getting on that roller coaster ride! Imagine how it felt when you saw that man or that woman that had a wonderful sex appeal while you were single! Or even better, imagine that man/woman that you first laid down with when you first had sex! Now, possibly compare this feeling to someone that has lived a life of disappointments and is afraid to tell her family about her down falls because everyone knew she would be the first lawyer in her family. Imagine the feeling she has to reveal such information. Such feelings could make the average person want to do one of the following things:

-A desire to want to lie

-A desire in wanting to hide from the world

-A desire in wanting to have suicidal ideations

-A desire in wanting to have cement style barriers to keep everyone out of her business

-To associate around people that are of similar issues

-To blame others for her mistakes

How Do I Date Constance?

Well, here's the tough part of the book. We have to discuss ways of being able to date one of the toughest women in the world; but is she really that bad? Think about it for a second, just like any other confrontational person, you have to really understand some of the reasons why a person is so confrontational. The next thing you would need to do is to decide if you're willing to deal with this type of person. Now, I can imagine it sometimes being easier said than done, but how would you know the success of trying if you don't lift of finger to even try? That's where the communication comes in.

Understanding Her

That's where sitting back and realizing if this is the person you would like to get to know comes in. Other things you would need to consider are being willing to help this person think of you otherwise than what she's been exposed to, help to understand the ways she prefers to be loved, and to not confuse it with the way you want her to be loved. There's a huge difference in what I just mentioned. Sometimes when we get into a relationship we tend to love and show to others the way were taught in doing so, but forget that not all women/men are the same way and may not be as receptacle in your love method. Your job is to understand HER ways of being loved so that you may continue it. Be mindful of that notion. Now, I want you think of how a patient feels after receiving surgery from the hospital. This person has to go under proper doctoring, resting, medication management and possible rehab. During this time, the person needs to be properly treated, taking it easy and placing self in areas where things are not to become worst; but better for the well-being of her. Think of that for a second. Now compare it to dating a person in real life. Some of us have been exposed to certain things in life and sometimes it can take a little time to re-adjust back; unless there's something or someone in the mix that's either helping or destroying the chances outside of their own ability to do better. On the flip side of knowing if you're ready to date this person, this woman has to also make sure that she's ready to date again as well. She has to realize that sometimes the mind/body needs rest after going through a devastating time in life. Rest is in place to help ease frustration and the mind as well. Without proper rest, the mind has no time in successfully adjust. Without proper emotional rest, some of what we've been exposed to will somehow be envisioned as a negative mindset towards every positive thing or individual that tries to enter her life. Something to think about people. If she decides to overlook her reasons for not taking a break for

Understanding Her

herself, she'll increase the chances of having unsuccessful relationships in the future. With that being said, be mindful of any of the following women you choose to date. Each and every woman I chat about in this book has a flaw, no matter how much glamor I may paint of them or the praise I may give; each one has the ability to be hurt and for her to have reasons for why she's the way she is. Be careful and treat people the way they morally prefer to be treated as it relates to their "Love Language."

> Learn to treat people the way they morally PREFER to be loved, not the way you were taught….

Boyish Brenda

Last, but definitely not least, we have "Boyish Brenda." Think about it for a quick second, in life we've always had that 1 or 2 female friends that could tell you more about sports then some of your own friends. We've seen those females in school or in the community that dressed more of a sporting figure then you would've coming fresh out the gym; and it made you question a few things. Also, we've met that one female that we unfortunately confused her with the image of a man, but with soft skin. That's right, meet "Boyish Brenda." Brenda is that female that has more male friends than usual, but is respected for doing so and not acknowledged as a "whore." Sometimes in life society will give that perspective of a woman that's frowned upon for having multiple male friends. In this day in age, society feels that a woman that has more than 5 active male friends is seen as a whore for some odd reason.

(Not true in my eyes, but that's another story for another day) Brenda is one that has grown up in a lifestyle that resembled the following attributes:

-Multiple male family members

-Several brothers

-A sport based family

-Both parents were very active in extremely aggressive sports

-One or more of the parents were of a homosexual preference

-Single parent home with just a father

-Viewing a parent interacting more with those of the same sex as that parent

-Being more involved in masculine style sports

-Has adopted the saying of "Females are too catty, and I prefer males as friends."

-Tends to be more competitive towards the male gender, as oppose to the female gender

-And many more...

With all of the things we have going on in society today, we have to be mindful and respectful of those that choose to think and/or prefer different things. With that being said, aren't we all different and prefer different things in life? Don't we all have differences of taste buds? What's the difference in someone preferring to have onions on a sandwich, versus someone that prefers extra mayo? In life we're taught to frown upon those that choose to date within the same sex, but expect society to accept us when he or she chooses to engage in infidelity ways. Hmmmmmm.......I'll let you see the hypocritical acts right now. Now, lets get on back to the purpose of this section;

we're focusing on "Boyish Brenda" and the ways on getting to know her from a completely different level. The next section we're focusing on is the "Don'ts of what to expect from Boyish Brenda."

What Are The Don'ts of Her?"

Just like the other sections, we would need to be mindful of things when considering the wrong doings of dating and/or getting to know this person. Some of those things are as follows:

-Possible moodiness

-Easily offended type of personality

-Very defensive

-Could present issues of role responsibilities

Possibly making her partner feel less of a man

Resistant towards being the "girly" type for her man

-"Not as effective" communication/skills as the average female may possess

-Could possibly scare a traditional male type who may prefer a specific type

-Could decrease the sex drive in a male partner

-Could take away from the traditional mindset of a guy wanting the nurturer type

-Could have so much in common that it could cause unnecessary issues

As confusing as it may sound for some, you would think that the more two people have in common that the more two people would get along. That's not always the case. Think on it for a second, the average couple in this day in age has many differences that draw one another to each other. When you have differences, it has the potential to draw one another to each other. Having differences makes the conversations more intriguing to the point of wanting to ask questions. Having differences encourages the chances of trying new things in life. Like for instance, you may have a partner in a relationship that has a fear of heights while the other enjoys it; so imagine the benefit of the person that's afraid of heights can learn from the person that isn't as afraid. Now on the flip side you can have two people that have a lot in common and it could present a better sign of happiness for one another for them to love and really enjoy. Sometimes having too much in common can make the average couple become more competitive. Sometimes having so much in common can cause both parties to begin comparing/contrasting things that they've done; whereas someone that isn't as competitive would be more eager to try some of those things that are different than one's own doings. In a previous comment, I chatted about her possibly taking away from the traditional mindset of a guy preferring the nurture type. What that means is that a man is exactly that, a man. A woman is exactly that, a woman. When you mix and mingle every now and then, at the end of the day both parties have their own gender differences. Of course Boyish Brenda possesses boyish intentions at times, but she will always have that mood transition while being a woman. Sometimes that can generate issues while trying to maintain a relationship at times. Think about it for a second, **what are some of the traits a man desires in a woman?**

-Someone touchy-feely

-A female they he can brag about while around friends, but can also be willing to associate with her friends/ girlfriends to get away

-Someone that can be very motivating

-Someone that can be submissive at times

-Someone that has reasonable similarities

-Someone that doesn't have as many sexual partners, but knows what she's doing in bed

-Someone that doesn't compete as much towards his ability to be an effective sportscaster.

-And much more….

Can I Date Boyish Brenda?

Here's the toughest question, is it possible to date "Boyish Brenda?" Hmmm good question. Some of the things you would need to address when dealing with this type of woman would be; being mindful of the things that separate her from being the "girly" type, if she's willing to compromise with her demeanor and/or personality, and if she's the one for you that you wouldn't mind dating with intent of getting to know. During this type of dating or any type of woman that you're considering; make sure you're agreeing to meet her 60% of the way. Just like any other woman, there's no better feeling knowing that you're man and/or partner that are willing able to accept you for who you are. The 40% is the desire or the effort in the compromise of Brenda learning to accommodate for her partner if possible. Something else to be mindful of is whether or not you're able and/or capable to accept her for whom she is. The things that I've mentioned are things that must not go unnoticed. Reason being is that there's no worse feeling being with a person whom you have no desire in getting to know and/or not having a legitimate liking for. On the flip side we tend to ignore the fact that "Boyish Brenda" may have similar things to us that maybe other women are either unable to accommodate, or to relate to.

Now, not to put a lot of negative inflictions on the "Boyish Brenda," but there's still hope in dating a woman with such tendencies. Just because she has boyish ways, doesn't mean she's unable to rock the hell out of a dress and make all the women around her a bit jealous. Just because she prefers boy shorts over a short skirt sometimes, doesn't mean she can't be the most attractive woman in the room. Lastly, just because she chooses not wear lipstick or watches some of the drama driven shows like others, doesn't mean she wouldn't love you like a woman would any less. So the real question now is "Are YOU ready for her to accept a date from YOU?

Just because she prefers boy shorts over a short skirt sometimes, doesn't mean she can't be the most attractive woman in the room

Below, I'm going to submit a nice size table that depicts what and how society views and/or expects a woman to be, versus how a boyish Brenda would be:

Understanding Her

Boyish Brenda	Becky Sue
More sports driven	Drama driven tv
Manly shorts	Short shorts
Boxer briefs	Thongs
Oils/Fragrance	Mist/Fragrance
Basic Hairstyle/Pony Tails	Frequent hairstyles
Rare make-up	Frequent makeup driven days
Jordans/Walking shoes	Heels, flats
Not as affectionate	More affectionate

Relationships are based on whether or not two parties can be willing to get to know one another, to understand one another in treating them the way they prefer to love, and to learn the most effective ways in building together as one. I'll let you decide if you would like to date "Boyish Brenda."

101 **Understanding Her**

"O"

Whew, 100 pages later and now we're at the "Occupation" side of things for the ladies. So lets get straight to the point then; our first lady of interest is the **"Independent Issabella."** Well of course we can name a load of independently driven positions that are out there, but I want you to remember that just because she's the independent type, doesn't mean that she's always financially successful. Sometimes we confuse the independent people with having all the money in the world, but in actuality she's the type that just prefers to do everything on her own; with hopes of her being super financially successful. So, lets chat about some of the independent Issabella occupations. Depending on if she's the financial type of independent woman, more than likely here are some of those job offers:

-Attorney
-Physician
-Nurse Practitioner
-Therapy
-Project Manager
-CEO
-Any type of managerial position
-TV Host

Now, to piggy back on a message I stated a second ago about the type that may not be in a financially successful status, this occupational status is something that one prefers to be independent, but from a subconscious form or fashion. You may not see the independence in the work place, but you'll see the independence is one's presentation to the world. What I mean by that is, one may want the world to see that things are on an independence level, but in actuality or in one's work ethics are a totally different ball game. Now, we have the next occupation for **"Debby Dependent."** This next person of interest is one of those "flies by the weight of the world" or the "where ever the wind blows" type of lady. By Debby being the dependent type, it's safe to say that she'll have a tough time coming into the fold with a job of her own passion. It's safe to say that Debby may have a strong desire to not even work if you ask me. It's safe to say that Debby may be in or on her 4th or 5th job this year and it's not even June yet. It's safe to say that Debby will more than likely be apart of one of the following job types that usually says temporary status:

-A job that she feels confortable in quitting as soon as possible

-Stay at home parent

-Professional students

-Lower level call center staff

-Adult club Setting

-Sometimes the Bar Tender

-A Flagger

-Positions with a less amount of benefits and low pay.

-A position with less responsibilities and/or obligations to be successful

With that being said, I want you to pay close attention to some of the things I've mentioned here. I want you to pay attention to the types of jobs this type of woman prefers. This type of woman thinks on that "Just Enough" mentality to attract others. Now, there are millions of guys that may prefer this type of woman, but my suggestion is to be both mindful and careful with playing your cards. Remember what I said, there's no need to complain if you've decided to choose either woman after already realizing the type of woman she's turned out to be. Next, we have a new occupation style of a lady; **Insecurity Levine.** This type of lady could be a bit tricky, but it's all about understanding your woman. Just like attempting to pass an exam in school, your first thing to do is to ensure that you've studied enough, to ensure that you've been given the right materials to be successful, and to ensure you that have had enough rest the night before to increase the chances of being successful on life. Now back to Levine. When dealing with someone that may not have the highest self esteem in the world, you have to play your cards right. With this type of person you have to be aware of her esteem level, the goals she has in life, and what types of things drive her in wanting to do better in life. For example, a person with super low self esteem may not be applying for law school anytime soon until she's developed a sense of comfort in her life or at least having developed confidence in speaking in front of crowds. Society will paint an image of someone with self-esteem issues or insecurity issues to have occupations that are of less importance or less value. Society will show that those with low self esteem or of low insecurity level will have positions that may not demand too much work that steps outside of her own person growth area. Now, I have met some that realize the insecurity levels of themselves to be low, but will do everything possible to accept things that are outside of one's scope just to prove to both the world and one's psyche that the sky is the limit and they can do better. Here are some of the positions you may see someone of the "Insecurity Level" be involved in:

-Small firms that are of 1-3 products

-Entry level house keeping positions that are of 1-3 responsibilities

-Secretarial style work

-Lower level security positions without weapons

-Front entrance restaurant style positions that are of less responsibilities

The premise of this section or at least any other occupational sections is to describe the intent behind each woman's purpose. As you can see, a lot of the jobs are dependent upon the woman's esteem level, her drive, and the desire to do better in life. I do realize that circumstances do arise at times in life, so it's expected that some may disagree with what I'm mentioning in this lovely book; but if I had a dollar for every time someone disagreed with me, I'd be a millionaire right now.

Next, we have **Conswella Control.** This very precious young lady is a force to wrecking with. Remember the key word in this type of person; CONTROL. This young lady had the ability to control a lot of situations in her mind, just to possibly apply it to her life and those surrounding her. When a person seeks and/or desires a lot of control, you'll tend to see them in positions that sometimes compliment that flaw or recognition. You'll sometimes see her in a position where she has full control, the ability to pass along her task to other people, or in a setting where some have records that may limit them on voicing too much of opinions that stand beside the controlling person. For example, if I know that you have a concerning criminal background, then 8 times out of 10 I'm going to keep you grounded, I'm going to ensure that you do not step out of line when addressing me, and I'm going to ensure that you follow any and all of my directions accordingly. Here's one thing to pay attention to as well with this type of woman; sometimes you'll see a woman that's very controlling but isn't in a controlled work environment where she can run things. Reason being is because her control issues aren't within the work environment, it's within a place some call home. Sometimes you'll see women that have no form of control in the home setting, but will come to work just to vent and control everything smoking with a badge and an ear to listen to her. Vise versa, sometimes you'll have a spouse that has no control in her job market as she requests, but will come home to her comfort zone just to fulfill that void. Some of us love the desire to control, but have no idea how to even control the ambition in being in control so we do it in a way that's comfortable to our belief system. Here are some of those places of employment you may see your woman involved in:

**-Department of Social Services
-Child Protective Services
-500 Fortune Companies
-Financial Companies
-Coaching Positions
-Therapy Style Positions
-Positions that are of a "Needed Basis."**

The premise of this type of woman is to seek the control aspect of things. Many would struggle in understanding and/or dealing with a woman of wanting much control, so that's why It's best to recognize these things from the jump and immediately make a decision as to whether or not you will proceed in dating her. Remember, you don't have that right to complain too much if you still choose to become as one with her.

Next, we have the preferred type of woman, "**Co-Co Dependent.**" This woman is much easier to explain than the rest. Think about it for a second, in life some of the most happiest couples are with those that compliment their personality, that are able to compliment them emotionally, and are more beneficial than the rest. The world views this woman as a supportive wife for sure. Now, lets focus more on the Co-Co Dependent place of employment. The Co-Co Dependent is viewed as someone that's very helpful, inspiring and uplifting to many. Consider the following places of enjoyment for her:

-Counselor

- **Coach**
- **Motivational Speaker**
- **Child Care Worker**
- **Crisis Center Worker**
- **Pastor/Preacher**
- **A Nurse**
- **Certified Nursing Assistant**

The premise of this type of woman is to show the world that there are still helpful and inspirational people left in the world. Many confuse the lack of trust and infidelity acts that are occurring as the notion of there being no more good people left in the world; not the case anymore!! I'll let you be the judge of that, because the world I live in says otherwise.

Next we have "**Constance Confrontation.**" This type of woman is one that you really have to be mindful and cautious of. My reasons for saying so are because this woman is expected to attack, to feel threatened, and to have her guard up at all cost. When we think of someone that's confrontational, we immediately think that she's either upset, not as content in her own doings in life, feels that her life is always compared towards everyone, or constantly having to live in a hostile place of comfort. When a person doesn't feel excited about their life, or doesn't agree with how things have gone with one's success plan, you have to be mindful that she's going to be more attracted to those that are in a similar status. With that being said, imagine what type of job this woman is considering applying for:

-Low paying Call Center Position

-Positions that require a load of information to be retained, to prove to others that she's intelligent

-Correctional Officer

-Security Officer

-Phone positions

Understanding Her

-A job of her least interest

-Insurance claims

-Attorney at times

-A job that she's constantly complaining about to others on a daily basis

-Telemarketing Jobs

-Debt collectors

With that being said, you have to be mindful of who you are choosing to date in this world today. Not everybody is ready for the commitment of dating. Not everybody is ready for the commitment of humbling self to successfully get to know other people.

Last but definitely not least, we have the **"Boyish Brenda" type.** When dealing with someone that's of a boyish mentality and it's appearing to be a woman, a lot of the times you'll see it where the female will tend to work at places where her masculinity side may begin surface. Sometimes you'll see the this type of woman working in a place where she's behind the scenes a lot. Sometimes you'll see this woman in a role where her presence or presentation isn't as required for being as vocal. Sometimes you'll see this woman in a isolative style job. At times you may see the total opposite. You may see her in a role where she's more of the vocal type role where a point has to be proven, or in a position where she fights for a cause. Sometimes you'll see this boyish style woman within the following workplace:

-A gym setting

-A sporting style place of employment

-Sometimes it's a job where she may work around a lot guys

-Positions that involves playing very active sports

-Positions that involves working out and/or lifting weights

-Rappers

-Security/Bouncer in the club

-Tattoo artist

This concludes the occupation category of the "How To Understand A Woman." Like I've stated before, you have to be mindful of the woman you decide to allow in your life. You have to be mindful of how to understand her, how to date her, and understanding how she can somewhat benefit who you are as a person.

"M"

Now, we must head on to the next part of the woman. This section will focus on some of the maturity areas of the woman species; but with a little twist in the "irrational vs rational" category. No matter the ethnicity, the gender, the heritage, or even the sex; we as people will be exposed to many different things in life that have the ability in tampering with how we function as people. Whether we've lived a lifestyle of unfortunate abuse, neglect, or even the lifestyle of the super wealthy; the world still has a way of offering a choice to either be irrational or rational towards things in life. Lets begin with several of the ladies we've discussed during this book.

Independent Issabella:

When we think of someone with the independent spirit in him or her, it makes us ponder on what she'll be willing to compromise on, if she'll be the type that'll look out for the best interest a lot of the times, or will she more so continue to look out for the best interest of herself. When dealing with independent style women as I've discussed, it'll tend to become an irrational vs rational competition for them. My reason for saying so is that this woman may view things from a financial and/or singular approach that she feels could benefit the family; whereas the party that's on the other end of the relationship may feel that

her decision was a bit lopsided and not even considered with both parties included. When dealing with the "Irrational vs. Rational" disputes with this type of woman, look forward in having these types of issues as each relates to the "Irrational vs. Rational" convos;
- a. **Financial**
- b. **Intimacy**
- c. **Savings**
- d. **Friends**
- e. **Social atmosphere**
- f. **Power struggles**

A lot of the issues will be the differences of both party's opinions. There will be times of attempting to debate over who's wrong, who's right, when one should take accountability, and who should decide on apologizing for things. When dealing with this type of woman, you have to be mindful as to how things are handled for the most part. You have to be mindful that this woman can and will handle certain situations in life different than what many of us are used to. This notion will tell you the most about her; hints the reasons we're going over the "Irrational vs. Rational" side of things. The independent type may not have the most desirable sexualized intentions in her relationship. Sometimes you may see where the independent type could be so focused on being independent on everything, that it takes away from a reasonable sex appeal towards everyone else. On the flip side, this woman could be the total opposite. This woman could demand so much independence that it increases her sex drive towards her partner. Something just thinking about that can causes those heated convos in relationships now days with women.

Some independent women may prefer you not to have any access to how she handles her money, which is often viewed as the irrational side of notions. You have some independent women that prefer not to address her issues with her significant others during tough times because she's been taught that it's a sign of weakness.

Understanding Her

Sometimes you may see the independent type of woman that may struggle in going off track with things in life that aren't going as how she originally has it planned. As you can see, the average independent woman may view things from one or fewer ways outside of how she thinks; whereas someone of a different make-up would view things completely different. As for the social life of this independent type, sometimes so much independence from others could decrease the chances of her having a reliable social life or even a load of friends. You'd be surprised the energy people lash away from when the vibe isn't mutual. These women will more than likely handle things from a "heart concept," as oppose to her mind. Statistics say that the majority of irrational decisions stem from thinking with your heart, as oppose to the mind. Being able to use your mind much more than other areas allows us to make much better and sound decisions. Being able to make decisions with your mind allows you to use sound judgment and to increase the chances of living a better life. Thinking with you mind is the same as the myth "gut feeling," whereas thinking with her heart is the "making the decision based on hurting someone's feelings."

Debby Dependent

And then we have the "Debby Dependent" type here. There's only so many ways this type of woman thinks from both the irrational side, and the rational side of things. In life what some view as irrational thinking, some of us view it as a way of life. Speaking in reference to "Debby,' some will view her as someone that may not be able to do too many things on her own, or at least with her very own confidence. Some may view her as someone that may struggle in accomplishing goals or possibly not having that inner motivation in wanting to have goals. Society view "Debby" as the irrational thinker due to being exposed to a life where she's unable to do much on her own. Society views this woman as someone that prefers to be the type from the early 30's and 40's where the woman couldn't contribute as much to the home and was dependent upon her significant other. Having considered these types of characteristics in a woman, it kind of makes you think about what's irrational to her, vs. what's considered rational to her as well. In speaking with several women that are of this category; some feel that allowing a man to be the head and to take care of all the house duties and responsibilities is enough. The opposing woman in the world may view that as someone with no backbone. Some women may view that as an excuse not to be successful. Some women may view that lifestyle as a way of someone wanting to control her. Other women may view such lifestyle as a woman with no values in life to do better. Of course some may view it as irrational, while other view it as a way of life. I'll let you be the judge of that one.

Insecurity Levine

Now we have the "Insecurity Levine" woman of interest. Sometimes in life we'll make decisions out of own belief system, while subconsciously choosing to avoid other options. In life we're faced with many different obstacles that are pretty heavy on our psyche; limiting us on the choice to adapt to a successful state of strength, or struggling to manage life's weaknesses. When we think of insecurities, we begin thinking of emotional limitations in life where things have happened that have been put on hold for growth within us. Insecurities are things that prevent us from moving forward in life. Insecurities are in place to assist us in doubting others, doubting the truth sometimes, and also keeping us from believing in ourselves. Insecurities are there to prevent or limit couples today on being able to trust one another; sometimes prior to couples even beginning to date. The real question now is, "What makes the irrational v rational conversation alive within this section of the book? Well, society has painted multiple portraits in life that's designed in deterring us away from making good decisions. Society has a way of convincing many that if someone cheats on you once, then the odds of others either like him or different from him will continue to do the same cheating episodes. Society teaches us that rational plays the role of always making the right decision and you'll be ok. The differences in irrational v rational plays that role of knowing right from wrong, and knowing how to apply the correct method of choice. Insecurity Levine in this instance has a tough time applying what she needs to be doing at times. Sometimes you'll find this type of woman being confrontational, displaying more signs of being dishonest, verbally abusive, and frequent issues with belittling others. Sometimes this woman has history of making more irrational decisions than any of the other 6 women that I've mentioned. This woman has multiple ways in how she displays her irrational v rational choices in life:

Irrational	vs. Rational
Low self esteem	*Higher self esteem*
Anti Social	*Loves people*
More health prob.	*Less health prob.*
Poor relationships	*Few bad relationship*
Argumentative	*Communicates*
Excuse giver	*Accountability*
Procrastinator	*A Go-Getter*

Irrational decisions will either make or break you. The real question now is," Will you make the choice to do better in life, or continues to work for those that are already planning to help them and their entire family in doing better with your help?

Understanding Her

Conswella Control

Next we have the "Conswella Control" type. This is the type that prides herself on dictating all situations. This is the person that gets a kick out of being in control of things at times. This is the person that'll exhaust all options to finagle situations to where it can only benefit them to say the least. This is the person that'll try and avoid all responsibilities in life just so they wouldn't have to take accountability. Make sure you're careful when dealing with this type of a woman. Now, lets get started on the "irrational v rational" side of things. What might be considered irrational to some, Ms Conswella would consider refusing to admit when she's wrong about something as rational. What might be considered irrational, Ms. Conswella might consider apologizing as a way of showing her weakness. What might be considered irrational to some, Ms. Conswella might consider embracing a person's weaknesses by using each one against the other person as a way to control the person of interest.

Make sure you're taking into deep consideration when deciphering as to whether you want to date this type of person. Of course we have some that are able to adapt to certain behaviors of her, or are able to balance such behaviors; but remember that life is filled with choices and you do not have to date anyone you do not like.

Co-Co Dependent

The "Co-Co Dependent" type is one like no other. This is the woman that has a wonderful understanding of irrational decisions, vs. having a better understanding of rational decisions. This is the type of woman that tends to think with her mind more than when she decides to think with her heart. This is the type of woman that thinks with a proper understanding of who she is, versus comparing herself to someone she thinks lives a great life. This is the woman that caters not only to the people that love her, but most importantly to the star player; herself. Meet "Co-Co Dependent." As you can see from the beginning to this portion of the book, this type of woman is one that's favored the most. Not necessarily by me, but by many that seek out good women. Not to say that this woman is better than anyone else in this book; we all have our very own demons, but I really want us to pay close attention to the type of woman that I'm discussing. I do realize that we don't ask for people to harm us. We don't ask for people to mistreat us. We definitely don't ask for people to cheat on us either. Sometimes in life we tend to process and/or handle things differently than the average woman now a days; the real question now is," How do you plan on handling things in the near future and how would you like for it to affect you?

Constance Confrontation

One of the last one's, but definitely not the least, we have Ms. "Constance Confrontation." This is the woman that feeds upon conflict, not conflict resolution. This is the one that feeds upon starting and/or keeping the relationship in drama as much as possible. This is the one that sometimes may not be as confident in her own self, so she attempts in bringing others down with her. This is the one that feeds upon animosity in others, to allow it to embrace who she really is. Now, imagine this type of woman while in a relationship discussing irrational vs. rational. I'll wait.....This may be the type that refuses to admit that she's wrong. This may be the type that refuses to end an argument because the principle of arguing intrigues her. This may be the person that has an extensive history of dating guys that cause nothing but drama in her life and maybe any guy that she meets in the future reminds her of just that guy. This could also be that woman that expects everyone to hurt or belittle her in the future so she prepares herself for that no matter what. With this type of woman, you have to be very careful when considering dating. Most importantly you have to be mindful that she's ready to get back out there and date again. There's no worst feeling being with a person who's either not ready to date again, or views the world as a threat to her. There's no worst feeling wanting to love someone, but everything about says run.

Boyish Brenda

Now, this one may be a little tricky. Reason being is because you're now dealing with 3 people; the female in the relationship, the significant other, and the boyish side of her. Already that's too many eyes in your personal business if you ask me. If any set of 3rd eyes should be apart of a relationship, it should be

God himself. Sometimes in life we allow too many people into our circle and it can become hostile. Too many times we allow unwanted or negative people into our lives that have no place in being there. Too many times we allow people into our circle that WE KNOW shouldn't be there; but we do it any way. With that being said on the "Boyish Brenda" contestant, please be mindful of who it is you're allowing into your life. Please take heed of the "dating phase" as a place of getting to know someone to see if you guys can make it to the big dance; not to automatically be there just because you guys are dating.

> Please take heed of the "dating phase" as a place of getting to know someone to see if you guys can make it to the big dance; not to automatically be there just because you guys are dating.

"A"

This section will focus on the addition of her. This section is about the type that these lovely women prefer, vs what they actually need.

Independent Issabella

When dealing with the independent issabella type, you have to remember the actual type of person she is; very ambitious, will more than likely consider herself first over everything, will more than likely make her own money, and will have you thinking your just a supplement to the relationship as oppose to her primary support system. The real question now is, "What exactly does her addition look like, or what exactly would be her type of guy?" Who on gods green earth would be a great fit for good ol Issabella? This will be interesting. Depending on how she's been raised and the circle that she keeps around her will tell it all. If she grew up in a lifestyle of helping the world, loving everyone, real family oriented but boujee at times; 7 times out of 10 you will see her conversing with guys that she may get a kick out of helping a lot . Helping a lot as in maybe she's making more money, she would prefer in him being a hubby home mate, or even someone she wouldn't mind in not taken over the "head of household." Another type that you might see within the addition of Issabella would be the type that can somewhat match her and her accomplishments. This type of woman was taught from jump street that those that fall into a similar financial category, those that can contribute just as much as she can, or someone that is of a popular status would be a great asset to her. Think about it for a second, each woman that I'm going to be speaking with you about will prefer those that she's been taught how to love. For example, imagine seeing and believing the way your mom was treated by her father. Imagine how you've seen your mom treat the father in the home. Imagine how your dad has constantly embedded into your mind as to how a guy should treat you. Imagine the roses your dad has given your mom out of love or of apologetic measures. Imagine how your dad treated your mom when he became upset and it led to domestic violence. Remember, the apple doesn't fall too far from the treat; the question now is, "What are willing to catch?"

Debby Dependent

This next woman will be pretty easy to explain. Well, when you look at the title of the name, you'll notice that she's the "Dependent type." This type is the same one that will seek in dating those that are of a financial blessing to her. She's one that may not have as many goals in life. She's one that may be looking for a "come up" as oppose to looking for ways to boost her business. Once again you have to be mindful of those that do not have as much going on in their lives. Some will view you as an asset, while others view you as a way to help US grow as one. There's a difference. Now, imagine the type that she prefers; she may have lived in a lifestyle where parents weren't as financially successful. She may have lived in a lifestyle where one parent shows history of depending on others to supply her needs. She may have been the person that only viewed guys with money as a way to move up in life. She could be the female that looks for those that can provide comfort for her for materialistic value. This woman needs a man that is wiling to provide more than just financial gain, but other business style ideas that can possibly motivate her to want to do better in life. This woman will need to be shown the importance of loving without the financial blessings. What she'll need to know how to do is to focus on "What if the money were to magically disappear?" This instance would really show the difference in how she loves, versus how fast she may walk out of the room. What she needs is someone that can dig deep into help psyche to create new heights of motivation so that she may learn the necessary ways in wanting to do better and to contribute more than what society has taught her in doing so.

Insecurity Levine

First off, she may just need a therapist first before anything!!! Just kidding. Like with any other woman being described in this book, we all have issues that have affected us over time. We all have unfortunately allowed the masses or negativity to affect us in our decision-making; the real question is, "How long will you allow it to affect you?" With this type of woman, she wants exactly what every other woman desires; to be loved and appreciated like no other. There's one thing different about this woman though;

she's been hurt more than usual which means she may need someone that's not as critical about who she is, and more positive. About this woman, she may need someone that's less domineering and more humble of her needs. With this type of woman, she may not need a ladies man, but more so someone that can place his multiple lady friends to the side for her where it doesn't distress her insecurities. This woman will need someone that can meet her where she is goal wise and take initial baby steps in moving forward successfully in life. Prior to that, he will need to ensure that she's ready to move past her own insecurities. With anyone, you can try to help a person in need but if she's not ready to change, then your efforts are just as good as the breathe you used in trying to help that woman.

Conswella Control

Now we have THE CONTROLLING TYPE! Whew, be careful with this one. Ol Conswella has things that have been placed in her life or have intentionally added to her life that have allowed her to desire to control anything that comes in her pathway. With this type of woman, you have to be mindful of her potential and intentions. With this type of woman you have to be aware that argument, manipulation, and signs of multiple demands that WILL come into play a lot of the times IF you allow them to. Now, I'm not going to market this type of woman as the worst; but what I will do is chat with you about what she deems as a good guy, and what she actually needs. This type of woman is one that'll either need someone she can belittle or control at times. This woman will need a partner that doesn't really have a voice to stand up for one's self. This type of woman will need a person that may not mind his woman or her to take charge or control over things. This type of person may want someone that she can have full throttle over to keep him or her from locating her deeply rooted insecurities. Pay close attention to the last thing I mentioned; some "Conswella Control" types seek out to be in full control sometimes because they fear the other half seeing who they really are. Sometimes one will attempt in controlling everything so that you may not see the real them or maybe they're even afraid for themselves to see the real them in themselves. Now, here's a little twist; some woman that demand so much control may have dealt with guys in the past that had nothing going for themselves, so maybe the woman felt obligated in taking over. Sometimes a woman with control issues may just want to make sure that you can actually take the lead without her doing it. Women are very difficult in understanding or even trying to read their minds. So, that would be tough in deciphering due to not knowing where the control mechanisms come from, or if she's willing to give up such antics to allow you to be the head. PAY ATTENTION and remind yourself as to what you like in a woman and what you do not like in a woman and make a decision from there.

Co-Co Co-Dependent

One of societies most favored women of all ages. Let me explain this one to you; sometimes when we're in an argument with those of our sexual preference, we turn it into a competition. Reason being is that we're seeking at either winning the argument, or winning to argument at all cost. But if you think about it, what happens to the other party that's on the receiving in? It's simple; they become the party that society calls a "loser." The real question now is, "Why place yourself in a situation with a person that views your opinion and/or suggestions as a last resort or even a "just in case I feel like it" category of sort. With the "Co Co Co Dependent" type, you'll begin to see where the rational side comes out much more than usual. You'll begin to see this person as being irrational as it relates to defending you in a heated discussion when the world knows that you're absolutely wrong. Reason being is that if someone will have your back through the tough times, then imagine how it would be when times are great. If someone is willing to support you even though you're dead wrong, imagine how they'll be when you're right!!! The co-co type is one that tends to look out for best interest in those that surround her, including herself. This woman is one that doesn't mind thinking outside the box, and possibly bringing other people with her. This woman doesn't mind working a "9-5" to support a temporary cause, whereas some may be afraid to because it looks like she's taking care of him. This woman pays more attention to her better half, than societies lesser 15 percentile. You'll understand it later.

Constance Confrontation

Meet the one and only "Constance Confrontation." This young lady is one you may have to duck and cover every once in while. When I say, I mean exactly that. Sometimes they'll be times where she'll attack when feeling threatened. There will be times where she'll feel that she hasn't reached her potential in life and will push that frustration and animosity on the closest thing surrounding her. Sometimes this person will fight on the notion because she thinks someone was belittling her. People, please be aware of this lovely lady. This type of woman has unfortunately been accustomed to things in life that have promoted her to feel guarded. This woman has been exposed to things in life that have made her feel like those surrounding her are threatening her. This woman in life has been exposed to things that has a way of triggering those deeply rooted issues that say, "Attack." This woman tends to have a tough time rationalizing during, before and sometimes after the struggle of life. This is woman tends to see things completely empty, until the mist clears and she begins seeing half occupied. This woman is simply just like everyone else; affected in a way that has and will touch her intentions in life. With that being said, make sure you're mindful of the things you see in the women you choose. There's no worst feeling being with someone that isn't for you, but you're trying your hardest to force it and it's not pure.

Boyish Brenda

Last but definitely not least, we have "Boyish Brenda." This young lady is sometimes seemed as the ideal type of lady for any and every guy. Reason being

Understanding Her

is that what guy wouldn't want his woman to know just as much about sports as he does? What guy would want a woman that can associate just as humorous around his friends as he does? What guy wouldn't want a woman that can mimic the entire lyrics to a song that only you and your buddies play together? Now, each of those traits is actually pretty reasonable; the question is "Will society allow these questions to stand in the way of a possible success story." With that being said, what about the rational vs. irrational thoughts of this type of woman? Now a days we have the boyish type that's able to "turn it on, and turn it off." What do I mean by that? I mean that we now have women that can play her role of being the motivator in the locker room, but isn't afraid of being Ms. Seductive in the bedroom. This type of woman could be the type that can teach you how to manage a bank account at one time, and end up showing you how she prefers her bra to fit in the morning. When it comes to the rational vs irrational terms, we have to be mindful that we're facing someone that's able to adjust both sides of the world that the world isn't used to seeing and/or accepting. We have to remember that the one's we socialize and party with in the lockeroom, may not be the type we prefer to sleep with at night; unless it's one of those super drunken nights that only the guys know about and have kept it a secret to this day.

"N"

The nurturing side of this book will be the difference in success in relationships, or the rate that causes unnecessary issues. As individuals, we sometimes think of the nurtures' as the woman that caters to not only her man, but also more than likely to others in her family. When society paints the picture of nurtures, it makes us think about the woman that caters the most to her children over anything. Society has continued to paint the image of women being the ones that provide the cleaning for families, attempts in handling all emotional based issues in the home and trying to keep the peace in the home while the man/masculine one works. In todays time things have changed for either the worst, or for the better. Some of us as guys look at women as someone that can cook, clean, give up incredible and hesitant free sex; but we forget about that our women have just as many needs as we have.

With the 7 women that we're chatting about in this book, I think it's safe to say that they may have different ideas or opinions on the term nurturing. For instance, imagine the nurturing quality the average **independent woman** may have:

Understanding Her

7 Types & Descriptions

Independent	-Keeping any and all things in order whether it be business, financial, materialistic content, or perishable items in the home. -May tend to use work as to why one is unable/unwilling to stay on track
Controlling	The type that will refrain from being as nurturing as possible. The type that constantly revert her work to others. Will develop

	ways in manipulating other.
Insecurities	May either look for reasons to avoid nurturing those surrounding her, or will give every reason to nurture due to the fear of some type of emotional issue
Confrontational	This is the type that'll find every reason not to nurture you or anything you stand for because it LOOKS a certain way.
Dependent	To be honest this woman could go either way; she could be the type

	that'll run at the site of doing good work in her relationship to keep you, or she could be the total opposite because she sees the $$ signs after doing nurturing things
Co-Co Dependent	Will cater to each and every person in your family, including you if she has to be loved .
Boyish Brenda	Moody when it comes to nurturing those that surrounds her. Will do it Monday thru Thursday, but the rest of the week the role shifts

Understanding Her

With that being said, it has been an honor explaining different things to you about the psyche/mentality of the woman overall. Of course I may not have thoroughly explained everything you may have considered, but I've gone over things from a man's approach thus far. I realize that you will begin to see and read about things in the book that may upset, offend, or event shock you like no other; but one thing I want you to realize is that in life we're unable to make everyone happy. There's only a select few in the world that the lord himself will allow time to hear what you have to say, how you have to say it, and what time is available for you and them to exchange the sayings.

Throughout this book, I've had the chance to deliver my thoughts and insights of what women mean and are to me; the rest is up to you. Remember, women have, will, and are going through things in life that have the power to deter them from being the wife you envisioned them to be. Just as much as us guys have been through things in life that may not have placed us in an image the world may want; the real idolization now is, "What choice will you make when it's time to decide on if she's the type for you or not?" I hope you've enjoyed my book thus far, and I pray this book finds it's way in the world's hand real soon. Thanks again, and be blessed….

Johnathan M. Clark M.S.

Marriage & Family Counselor

www.Datedocta.com

"Adjusting Hearts, One Mind At A Time."

How to stay in contact with me:

 John Datedocta Clark

 The_Datedocta

 www.Datedocta.com

 Datedocta@gmail.com

Be blessed...

www.ingramcontent.com/pod-product-compliance
Lightning Source LLC
Chambersburg PA
CBHW070527010526
44110CB00050B/2171